CELTIC KNOTS
for
BEADED JEWELLERY

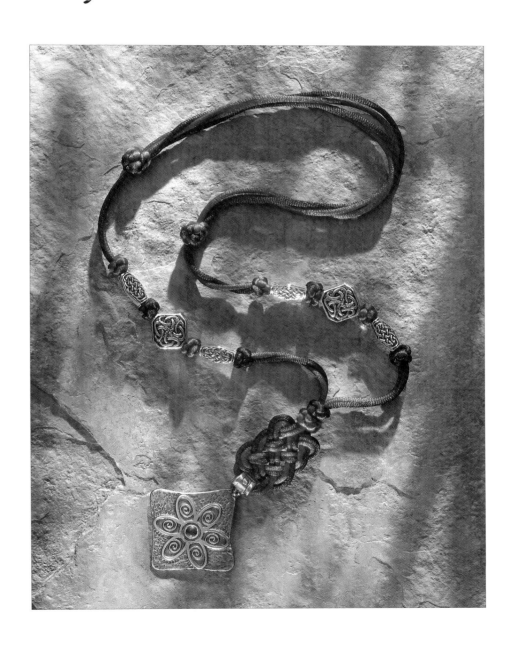

CELTIC KNOTS *for* BEADED JEWELLERY

Suzen Millodot

Gill & Macmillan

Published in Ireland 2006 by

Gill & Macmillan Ltd
Hume Avenue, Park West, Dublin 12
with associated companies throughout the world
www.gillmacmillan.ie

ISBN 0 7171 4048 2

First published in Great Britain by Search Press Limited,
Wellwood,North Farm Road, Tunbridge Wells, Kent TN2 3DR

Text copyright © Suzen Millodot 2005

Photographs by Roddy Paine Photographic Studios; John Liddle,
Cardiff (page 9); Simon Hind Photography, Cardiff (author's
photograph and step-by-step photography on pages 65–66).

Photographs and design copyright © Search Press Ltd 2006

Suppliers

If you have difficulty in obtaining any of the materials and
equipment mentioned in this book, then please visit the Search
Press website for details of suppliers: www.searchpress.com

You are also invited to visit the author's website:
www.chineseknots.com

Alternatively, you can write to the Publishers at the address above,
for a current list of stockists, including firms who operate a mail-
order service.

Publisher's note

All the step-by-step photographs in this book feature the
author, Suzen Millodot, demonstrating how to tie Celtic
knots and how to make jewellery using Celtic knots.
No models have been used.

Manufactured by Classicscan Pte Ltd, Singapore

Printed in Malaysia by Times Offset (M) Sdn Bhd

*Special thanks to Black Dragon Crafts in Wales for supplying
the beautiful Celtix beads and pendants used in many of the
projects in this book.*

*I would also like to thank several members of the
International Guild of Knot Tyers for their inspiring books,
namely Stuart Grainger, Skip Pennock and Eric Franklin.
From their books I learned about several very ancient and
attractive traditional knots (Turk's Head knots, chains, woven
flat knots and interlaced knots) that are in fact Celtic in style.*

*I am also indebted to my husband Michel for his constant help
and encouragement, not forgetting all the delicious meals he
cooked while I was working away on my knotting board!*

CONTENTS

INTRODUCTION 6

A brief history
Celtic interlace and knotwork

MATERIALS AND EQUIPMENT 12

Cords
Beads, pendants and findings
Other items

PREPARING CORDS 16

Calculating lengths of cord
Cutting and sealing cord ends
Dyeing cords

TYING KNOTS 19

BUTTON AND BRAID KNOTS 20

Button knot necklace
Braid knot necklace

PLAITS 30

Three-stranded plait
Four-stranded plait
Plaited necklace with beads
King Solomon's plait necklace
Four-strand plaited necklace with pendant

TURK'S HEAD KNOTS 38

Turk's Head bangle
Flat Turk's Head pendant
Turk's Head ring

FIGURE OF EIGHT CHAINS 46

Figure of eight chain bangle
Horizontal figure of eight chain
Horizontal figure of eight chain necklace

INTERLACED KNOTS 54

Celtic cross
Circle of Life earrings
Triangular knot earrings
Two heart brooch
Josephine knot necklace
Celtic square knot necklace
Rectangular Celtic knot necklace

INDEX 80

INTRODUCTION

When I moved to Wales and saw Celtic knot designs for the first time, I was fascinated by their flowing curves and repetitive patterns. They had the appeal of a puzzle, which one wants to look at again and again to try and visually follow and even unravel the design. They were to be found illustrating manuscripts, carved in wood and stone, enamelled and etched on to metal, impressed into clay, embroidered on to cushions, batiked and printed on to fabric and even burned as designs in wood. However, it was impossible to find a three-dimensional Celtic knot actually tied with cord or string.

A few years later we moved to Hong Kong. There, to my delight, I discovered Chinese knots, which are very decorative. Tied with a special cord for knotting, they can be combined with beads and are perfect for making jewellery. I learned how to make these knots and have been making and exploring the art of knot-making ever since. Now I have come full circle. Having moved back to Wales, my fascination with Celtic knots has been revived. However, this time I have my experience with other decorative knots to help me create real, three-dimensional Celtic knots.

Did real Celtic knots ever exist in the past? We shall never know, as the cords and string that would have been used to make them would not have survived the passage of time. However, there are many ancient decorative knots in existence which definitely are Celtic in style, being interlaced and plaited in a very similar way. They are very attractive and yet are relatively unknown to artists and teachers in closely allied fibre arts such as weaving, crochet and macramé. They certainly deserve to be revived and used with the colourful cords and beautiful beads that are so readily available today. Until now, these knots could only be found in books and journals for sailors and dedicated knot-tyers. I have searched them out, simplified the descriptions of how to tie them and used them to re-create Celtic knots in three dimensions which will be perfect for the creation of surprisingly modern, stylish jewellery.

Opposite
This necklace
(see pages 72–74) combines a
Celtic square knot with Celtic beads
and a circular pendant.

A brief history

The Celtic civilisation began to flourish more than 2000 years ago. It is thought to have originated in Central Europe, but its influence spread throughout the continent to Northern Europe. The Celts' artistic sense favoured decoration and pattern over mere representation. Celtic design has a very distinctive style, which has stood the test of time and is as admired today as it was centuries ago. It is typified by its exuberant curves and fluid, finely balanced asymmetrical patterns, stylised leaf and flower patterns and animal motifs, spirals, diagonal key patterns and intricate knotwork and interlacing. Another feature of Celtic artists and craftsmen is the love of strong colours. The ancient Celts were skilled craftsmen, and their artefacts that remain are of excellent quality. Unfortunately, their beliefs and ideas have been lost down the centuries, so what we know of them is mainly through their art and design. Therefore, we have very little mythology to attach to their artwork and the ancient pagan symbolism is almost lost to us. However, the Christian Celts lost no time in adapting the designs and using them to illustrate their own sacred manuscripts.

The designs which interest us for this book are chiefly the interlaced designs developed around the sixth century AD by Christian monks who used the curving, swirling patterns based on the ancient Celtic La Tene period (about 500 BC). By the early centuries AD, the Roman Empire had extended into most of Eastern Europe and Roman culture had overtaken that of the Celts in both Central and Eastern Europe. However, Celtic creativity had remained in the more western regions of Europe: the Romans had not reached Ireland or Scotland, and it was here that Celtic art and design survived intact, and the Christian monks were able to use the decorative forms as inspiration for ornamenting their manuscripts.

If you like Celtic knotwork, you are in good company. Famous artists such as Michelangelo, Leonardo da Vinci and Albrecht Durer all used Celtic knot designs in their paintings. Henry VIII has Celtic interlace borders on his cape and sleeves in a portrait by the School of Holbein. It is believed that the wonderfully sinuous Celtic La Tene designs also inspired the Art Nouveau designs of the late nineteenth century.

Opposite
A Celtic cross from a churchyard in St Fagans, Wales. A wonderful example of the combination of exuberance and control in Celtic knotwork. Note the button knot in the centre.

Celtic interlace and knotwork

Interlaced plaits were also used as decoration by the ancient Egyptians, Greeks and Romans, but these were plain plaits without any modification whatsoever. It was the Christian Celts who devised how to make new patterns from a simple plait by making breaks in the interlacing, and thereby creating more complicated designs. In the construction of patterns, each segment acts as a boundary in which the plait design is contained. It is these boundaries that change the designs from simple plaiting into interlaced knots. It is the boundary, or shape, which we are going to explore in the construction of our Celtic knots in three dimensions.

For readers who are interested in knowing more about the Celts and their art, there are many beautifully illustrated books describing their fascinating history. Interest and appreciation of Celtic art was greatly enhanced in the twentieth century, in fact there has been a modern Celtic revival. In the twenty-first century, the Celtic spirit is a stronger creative force than ever and many talented artists are continuing to produce beautiful work in the Celtic style.

Celtic designs have a magical, mythical quality. The animals are the stuff of legends, with wings and snakes' heads and elaborate, impossibly swirling tails. The plants are so stylised that they could not be identified in any botanical manual. The knots are similarly magical. If a practical knot-tyer examines the illustrations carefully, he or she will find that many of them have pointed loops, and 'floating' spirals and curves, which would never be able to maintain their shapes in three dimensions. This is, of course, part of their beauty, but from a purely practical point of view we will have to get down to basics and use the simpler plaits, braids and interlaced patterns. When adapting the forms, I made a rule for the knots that as far as possible they would be 'self-supporting', in other words they would not need to be attached to anything else to keep their shape (for example, sewn or wired on to a separate piece of fabric). There will be one exception and that is beads! If a bead, pendant or a finding is needed to reinforce the knotting, then all the better, as they will enhance and complement the beauty of the jewellery.

10

MATERIALS AND EQUIPMENT

Cords

I use cords in several different materials, both synthetic and natural. It is better to use a cord at least 1mm in diameter to show up the decorative knot; for jewellery a 2mm diameter cord is the thickest you will need. There is a special satin cord made especially for decorative knotting, which comes in many colours and looks smooth and silky although it is made from nylon or rayon. It has the perfect requirements for knotting: it is not too stiff, but firm enough to hold the shape of a loop without flopping. A good quality one will stand up to a good deal of handling without spoiling the appearance, a very important requirement for making elegant jewellery. It comes in both 1mm and 2mm thicknesses and is sometimes called rattail, a rather ugly name for a beautiful cord!

Another good cord is one produced for macramé. It is finely braided and is available in 2mm thickness and lots of colours. These days it is usually synthetic.

A selection of cords.

Cotton cord also comes in 1mm and 2mm diameter and knots very well. It is usually waxed so it will withstand moderate handling and does not stretch. It is available in a good choice of colours (although many stockists only have brown, neutral and black – we need to nag them to keep more colours!) Unless you are lucky enough to have a store nearby that sells these cords, you will have to order them by mail.

Nylon cord is available in white from hardware stores in 1mm and 2mm thicknesses. I like to work with it and I use an easy microwave method to dye it in an array of permanent colours; instructions are on page 18.

Leather cord looks lovely but the coloured leather does not withstand much pulling into shape. However, it is good for simpler knots.

Beads, pendants and findings

As time goes on, there are more and more beautiful beads available, both in bead shops and by mail order. There are advantages in buying your beads either way: it is enjoyable to browse in a store and examine the beads for details, and to determine the size of the holes, compare beads and see how they look next to other beads. On the other hand, it is also good to browse through a mail order catalogue at your leisure. One very important thing to look out for when ordering by mail is determining the size of the hole: is it large enough for the cord you intend to use?

Pendants often have larger holes and loops to suspend them and there is a huge variety available.

The same goes for findings. Since knotted jewellery tends to be bold in style, the chunkier, more unusual findings usually suit it better.

I often buy beads or old necklaces from second hand and charity shops. It is a matter of luck what you find, but there are some unusual pieces out there waiting to be discovered! Market stalls have some original ethnic jewellery and beads that are just asking to be combined with beautifully bold and colourful knots.

A selection of pendants shown with a finished necklace.

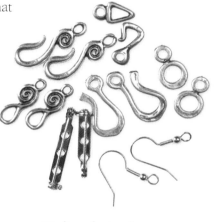

Findings for jewellery making.

An array of beautiful beads. Some beads can be bought as necklaces and re-used for your own designs.

13

Other items

Scissors Your scissors need to be good quality and very sharp to give a nice clean cut to the cord so that it is easy to thread through the beads.

PVA glue This is very good for stiffening the ends of the cords, making a stiff 'needle' to thread through the beads. It is also useful for strengthening the finished Celtic knots. If you paint on a diluted solution (one part glue to nine parts water), it will not darken the colour too much.

Paint brush For painting on the PVA glue. Buy a good enough quality not to shed hairs on to your handiwork.

Sticky tape Transparent tape is used to stiffen the ends of the cord to put through beads with nice large holes. This method is quick and easy but it does increase the thickness of the cord end.

Lighter This is used to seal the ends of synthetic cord to stop it fraying.

Thread zapper This is a fairly new product on the market and works well on thinner synthetic cords. It is battery operated and quickly heats up to cut and seal the cord in one go, giving a very neat, clean finish.

Cork mat Ideal for pinning your knot in progress as you follow the knot pattern. I use a beanbag tray with a piece of cork attached to it as it is easy to keep at a comfortable angle for working on.

Pins Used with the cork mat.

Tweezers Fine tweezers can be very useful for pulling cords through narrow gaps. They must have rounded ends and a gentle gripping surface to grip the cord without damaging it.

Instant glue gel The gel type of instant glue is easier to control than the liquid. A tiny droplet of glue gel holds the cord in place and will not spread on to surrounding cords, discreetly securing your finished knot.

Epoxy glue Useful for general jewellery tasks like gluing rhinestones or brooch backs.

Bead reamer This is so useful! Two needle files and a 45° hole smoother are stored in the handle for when you need to enlarge and smooth the bead hole. Do not forget to clean the filing surface frequently with an old toothbrush to keep it working efficiently.

Needle A tapestry needle with a large hole and a smooth, blunt end is very useful for weaving the cords over and under each other (for making the heart brooch on page 66 for example) and also for threading the cords back through a button knot to finish a necklace.

My beanbag tray with a cork mat attached to it.

Pliers and wire cutters Although we are working mainly with cords, pliers are very useful for dealing with findings. Two pairs of needle-nosed pliers are needed for opening jump rings, wire cutters are required for shortening headpins and round-nosed pliers are needed for creating round loops in wire for earrings or pendants.

Nail polish Very useful for stiffening the ends of cords for threading when the ends do not need to be very stiff. Quicker drying than PVA glue.

Cardboard cylinder A 7cm (2¾in) diameter piece of cardboard tubing cut from a tube (normally used to mail posters) is approximately wrist size and is used to make the Turk's Head bangles on page 38.

Tape measure Use this to ensure that you start off with enough cord to finish a project.

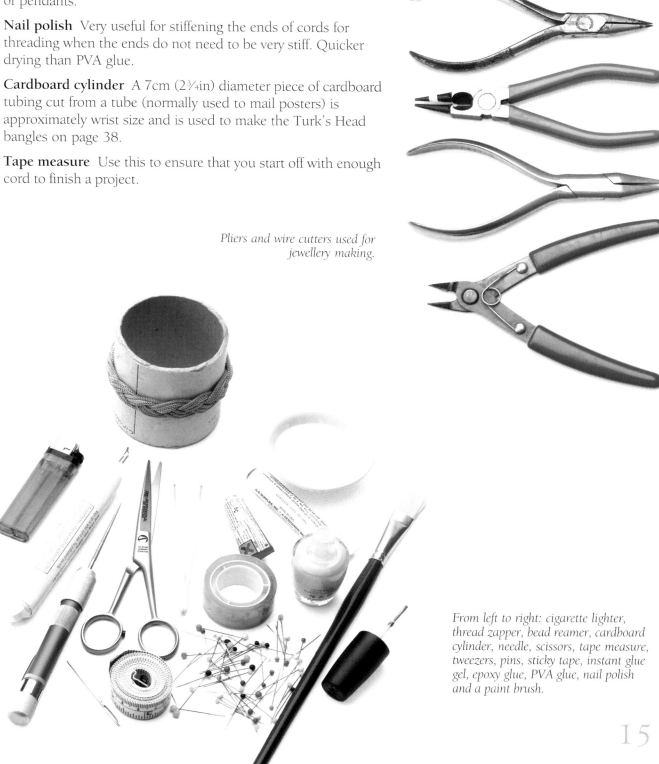

Pliers and wire cutters used for jewellery making.

From left to right: cigarette lighter, thread zapper, bead reamer, cardboard cylinder, needle, scissors, tape measure, tweezers, pins, sticky tape, instant glue gel, epoxy glue, PVA glue, nail polish and a paint brush.

PREPARING CORDS

Before you start making projects, you need to learn how to prepare cords.

Calculating lengths of cord

One of the most puzzling things to work out before you start a knotted project is how much cord will be needed to complete it. Often the cord required is much longer than you would have imagined. For example, the Turk's Head bangle on page 38 is made around a cardboard cylinder that is less than 7.5cm (3in) in diameter. Yet the amount of cord required to make the bangle is actually about 3m (118in); much more than you would think. The average length of a short necklace is approximately 45cm (18in) and the length of a long necklace is at least 70cm (28in). However, for both of these I usually start with 3m (118in) of cord, as at least 30cm (12in) of extra cord will be needed to be able to tie the last knot on each side. So it is better to err on the long side to be sure of being able to finish the project. You will notice that I have frequently mentioned the length of 3m (118in). If you see some particularly lovely cord but are not sure which project you will use it for, always buy at least 3m (118in) to be sure of having enough. Details of the length of cord needed are given at the beginning of each project.

Necklace lengths
The following table lists the average length of different types of necklace.

Choker	40cm	(16in)
Necklace with fastener	45cm	(18in)
Necklace without fastener	70cm	(28in)

Cord lengths for knots
The following table shows the approximate length of 2mm cord required to tie single knots.

Button knot	8.5cm	(3½in)
Sliding button knot	9.5cm	(3¾in)
Double button knot	25cm	(10in)

The following table shows how to determine the total length of 2mm cord required to make an 80cm (32in) necklace with one double button knot, ten single button knots and two sliding button knots.

Length of necklace	80cm	(32in)
Double button knot	25cm	(10in)
Ten button knots	85cm	(34in)
Two sliding knots	19cm	(7½in)
Allowance for tying the sliding knots	60cm	(24in)
Total length	269cm	(107½in)

It is better to have too much than too little, so I would add a small allowance for possible additions and cut a 3m (118in) length of cord.

Cutting and sealing cord ends

The cord will be easier to thread if the end has been cut on the diagonal with a sharp pair of scissors.

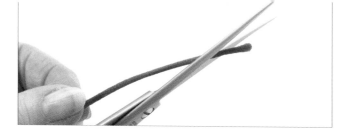

The cord ends need to be sealed to prevent fraying and as they are too thick to thread on a needle, they must be stiff enough to be able to pass through a bead easily. In a way, you will be transforming the end of the cord into its own stiff needle. There are several ways of doing this. The preferred method is to saturate the end with **PVA glue**, as shown. If the hole in the bead is uneven it is possible to cut a thin slice off the side of the stiffened cord end to make it thinner, to coax it through the bead. Actually, I have made some necklaces with beads made from semiprecious stones and have spent more time getting the cord through uneven holes than I spent tying the knots!

The second method is to use **nail polish** to stiffen the ends. It is not as stiff as PVA but dries quickly and is good enough if the holes are nice and large.

Use a small paint brush to apply the PVA glue to the cord. Use as much glue as the cord will absorb, all around, and up to 2.5cm (1in) from each end of the cord. Support the wet ends so they are not touching anything, then leave them to dry for at least an hour (longer for slow-drying glues) until the ends are very hard. Now cut the ends again to make sharp, needle-like points.

Sticky tape is another quick method, but it makes the ends thicker, so the holes must be larger than the cord thickness to allow the cord through.

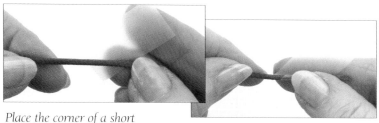

Sealing the cord end with nail polish.

Place the corner of a short length of sticky tape under the cord . . .

. . . then roll it round the cord with your finger and thumb.

You can also use a **lighter**. Place the end of the cord in the flame (do not apply the flame to the cord) for a fraction of a second, but no longer, or the end of the cord will become an ugly brown knob.

There is a new item on the market which does a good job of cutting and sealing synthetic cords all at once; it is called a **thread zapper**. It will cut thin cords very quickly, though thicker cords take longer, and it is a good way to avoid using a lighter. It is battery operated, heats up in seconds and cuts the cord cleanly. I find it most useful at the end of a project when I must cut the cord and seal it without spoiling the adjacent knot. It finishes the end neatly without the ugly dark knob which can result from using a lighter for too long.

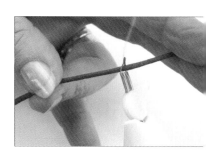

The thread zapper in action.

Dyeing cords

Although there are cords available in lots of colours, actually tracking them down can be very difficult! If you know how to dye the cord using the exact colour you want, you can create jewellery to your specific requirements. Nylon and rayon (also known as acetate or viscose) take dye very well, and the colours are as washable and permanent as any store-bought cord. Other synthetics, e.g. polyester, only dye to pale shades. Use multipurpose dye, which needs to simmer in hot water. I have found that it works perfectly in the microwave oven and is very quick and simple to use in this way. Note that the cotton cord used for knotting is waxed and will not take dye.

Method

You will need a large heatproof glass jug, a spoon, an old newspaper to protect the kitchen counter and rubber gloves. Wear old clothes or an apron. Wrap the cord around your hand to make a loose hank and secure it with a small piece of cord loosely tied around it.

1. Put 600ml (20 fluid ounces or 2½ cups) of very hot water into the jug.

2. Add ¼ tsp of dye and ½ tsp salt. Stir to make sure the dye powder dissolves completely.

3. Immerse the cord into the dye solution. Stir gently to make sure the cord is thoroughly saturated with dye solution.

4. Place in the microwave oven. Since ovens vary so much, it is not possible to give the power needed for your particular oven to keep the solution simmering. It will be a low or medium setting as you definitely do not want the solution to boil over.

5. After five minutes, check the colour and stir the dye. Most manufacturers recommend dyeing for twenty minutes, but it seems to dye much more quickly in the microwave.

6. When you have achieved the colour you want (do not forget it looks much darker when wet) remove the cord from the solution, rinse it and leave it still wound up flat on the newspaper to dry.

Dyeing tips

If you start with the solution lighter than you hope for, you can add more dye powder after five minutes. If on the other hand it is too dark, you will have to remove the cord, rinse and leave it to dry on the newspaper (still wound in a hank) and start again with a fresh piece of cord and a diluted dye solution. When I dye something, it usually turns into a dyeing session and I end up with about five different shades of cord. These are very useful for knotting, as closely related shades look very good side by side in Celtic knots – they add texture and depth to the design.

TYING KNOTS

One of the features of Celtic style knots is that the method of weaving the cords gives an alternate 'over and under' pattern. Once you have the knot pattern to follow, the concept is fairly simple. However, the over and under pattern only becomes obvious after you have finished. While you are working on it there are many gaps in the design as the cord changes direction frequently, and this is where it is so easy to go wrong! So, when you are beginning one of the more complicated knots like the heart knot on page 65, make sure you have no distractions and concentrate fully on what you are doing! Once the first cord has completed its pathway, it is easy to add the second or third cords, then you can relax and enjoy weaving the design. Always start the second and third cords in the same place as the first one, otherwise it is impossible to tighten it. Tightening the knot is fairly straightforward as you follow the pathway of the cords to tighten it. You sometimes have to repeat this several times to make the knot as tight as you wish and it has to be done gradually to keep the shape even.

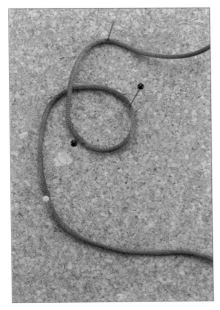

Pinning the cord to a cork mat helps maintain the shape of the knotting.

As the knot starts to take shape, add more pins as needed.

Tighten the knot gently and slowly, removing the pins when necessary.

BUTTON AND BRAID KNOTS

These are two basic knots that you really need to learn. It would be very difficult to make a knotted necklace without the button knot, as it is such an elegant and useful knot for finishing and hiding the ends of the cords. The braid knot is a very quick way to embellish a necklace or bracelet using just a few beautiful beads.

Button knot necklace

This knot is best known as a Chinese button knot. However, its round shape is typical of Celtic style, and its endless cyclical design represents the eternal cycle of life in Celtic symbolism as well as in Chinese Buddhist symbolism. It is an incredibly useful knot for making jewellery. This necklace is finished with Keren's sliding knot, making the necklace adjustable and very versatile.

You will need

3m (118in) 2mm braided cord
One large decorative ceramic bead
Six glass beads
Fourteen small gold filler beads
Brass hook and
eye closure

1. Seal the ends of the cords, place the bead in the middle of the cord and secure its position with pins.

2. On the right-hand side, thread on a small gold filler bead. Remove the pin.

3. Hold the bead and cord with your left hand and make a loop with your right hand.

4. Make another loop in front of the first one to create three spaces.

5. Insert the cord down into the first space on the right-hand side.

6. Bring the cord up through the centre hole.

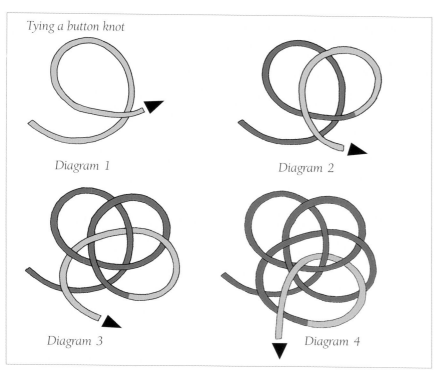

Tying a button knot

Diagram 1

Diagram 2

Diagram 3

Diagram 4

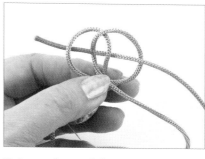

7. Insert the cord down again through the space on the left-hand side.

8. Pull the cord through but just enough to make a third loop on the right.

9. Bring the cord round to the right side and insert down into the new loop.

10. Bring it back up through the centre hole above your thumb.

11. Pull the cord through.

12. Pull the two ends gently to make the knot. Guide the knot towards the right side otherwise it becomes 'inside out'.

13. Pull the knot tight and pull the loops through one by one until they are flat against the knot.

21

14. The button knot should look like this.

15. Button knots always end up about 10cm (4in) away from the position you want them in. Examine the cord between the bead and the knot and find which loop it becomes on the other side of the knot (see the diagram below).

16. Pull this loop until all the cord is pulled through the knot and it is next to the bead (see diagram).

17. Pull the next loop through in the same direction (see diagram 4). Continue until all eight loops have been tightened.

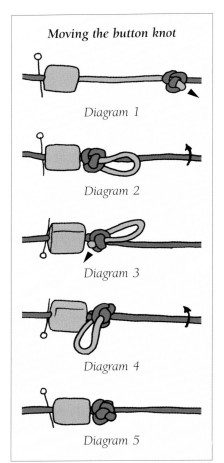

Moving the button knot

Diagram 1

Diagram 2

Diagram 3

Diagram 4

Diagram 5

18. Adjust the knot until you are happy with it; you will have to go round all the loops again to tighten the knot fully. There are no short cuts!

19. Add another gold bead on the other side of the knot, a blue glass bead and another gold bead.

20. Add gold beads, a button knot and a blue glass bead on the other side, so that the necklace is symmetrical.

21. Add a button knot, another blue glass bead flanked with gold beads and a button knot, then another blue bead with gold beads and a final button knot. Repeat this sequence on the other side. Thread on the closure about 10cm (4in) away from the knot.

Tying a sliding button knot

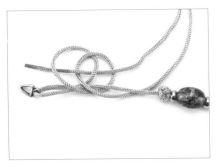

22. Take the end of the cord underneath itself.

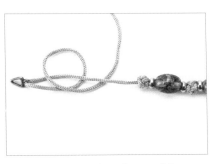

23. Loop around in front of the cord and up behind it again.

24. Loop around again in the same way and underneath the holding cord again. You are making a button knot in exactly the same way as pages 20–21 but looping it around the holding cord to create a sliding button knot. See the diagram above.

25. Thread the end of the cord into the first loop, up through the centre and down through the last loop.

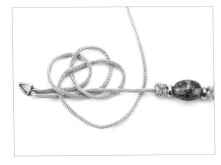

26. Pull the cord through to make a third loop, then back to the right and underneath the cord again. Note that all the loops coming up are behind the holding cord and all those going down are in front of it.

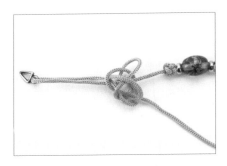

28. Tighten the knot, nudging it towards the right, otherwise the knot will be inside out.

27. Thread the cord down through the first loop and then up through the centre again.

29. Your finished button knot should look like this. It will slide up to the left to make a longer necklace and to the right to make it shorter.

30. When you are satisfied that the length is correct (you may have to move the knot), trim off the end with the thread zapper or use scissors and a lighter to seal the end.

31. Repeat steps 21–30 with a hook closure, on the other side of the necklace (see the diagram below). Adjust the length of the sliding knot to match the other side.

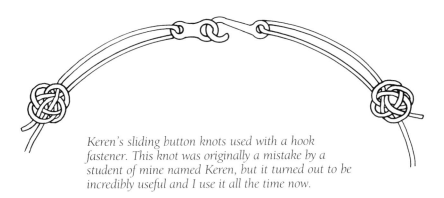

Keren's sliding button knots used with a hook fastener. This knot was originally a mistake by a student of mine named Keren, but it turned out to be incredibly useful and I use it all the time now.

Opposite

You can achieve many different looks using the simple button knot. All the necklaces shown have adjustable sliding knots, making them extremely versatile.

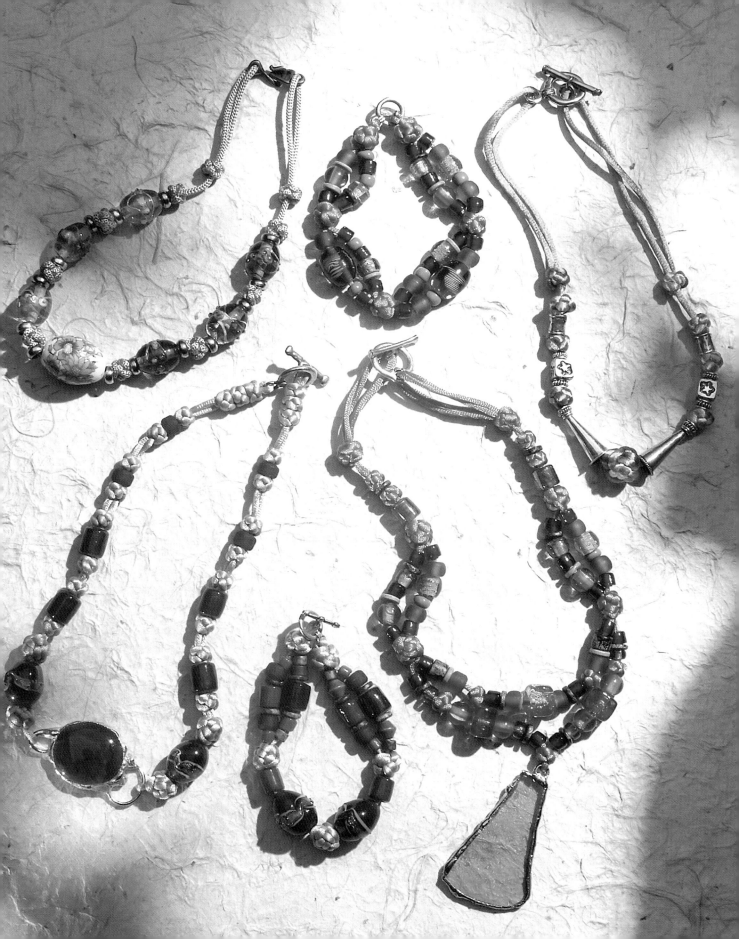

Braid knot necklace

The pattern of this knot is a basic pattern used frequently in Celtic design, and it is a quick and effective way to make a short, decorative, interwoven braid between beads and button knots. It is much more attractive and stable when the cords are doubled.

You will need

Two pieces of natural cotton cord, 3m (118in) each

Three large and two small painted wooden beads

Fourteen brass hexagonal nuts

Four brass flat washers

Brass hook and eye closure

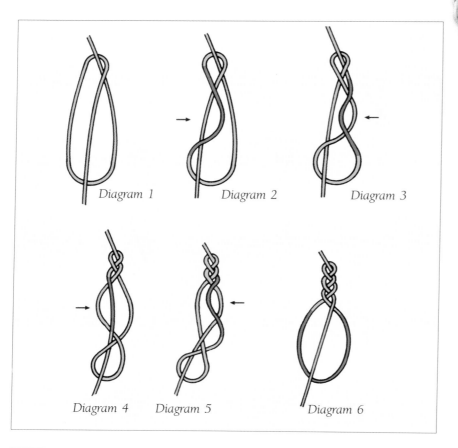

Diagram 1   Diagram 2   Diagram 3

Diagram 4   Diagram 5   Diagram 6

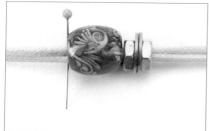

1. Thread two separate cords through a large wooden bead and secure the position with a pin. Thread a brass hexagonal nut, two brass washers and another brass nut on the right-hand side.

2. Use the doubled cord to make a button knot following the instructions on pages 20–21.

3. Tighten the knot partially. The cords should all be parallel, but you may find (as shown above) that they are not. If not, untwist them until they are parallel.

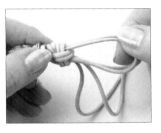

4. Loosen the knot and pull through the loops to move the knot closer to the bead, following the directions on page 22.

5. Your finished knot should look like this.

6. Add brass nuts, beads and button knots as above. Notice that the second and third button knots are smaller as only one cord was used to tie the knot around the other cord – see directions on page 23. Although this knot will not have the space to slide, it is tied in exactly the same way as a sliding button knot.

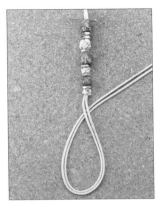

7. Pin the necklace into place on a cork mat and loop with two cords together around and under as shown.

8. Bring the cords down on the right and across to the middle; see diagram 1.

9. Start plaiting using the cords on the left-hand side, by bringing them into the middle – see diagram 2.

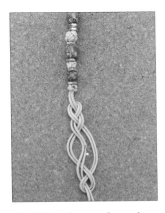

10. Take the cord on the right-hand side and bring it to the middle to continue the plait – see diagram 3. Continue plaiting by bringing the cords on the left to the middle as in diagram 4. You will notice that a mirror image of each crossing will form at the bottom of the knot (see diagram 5). These must be uncrossed as you go along.

11. Undo these unwanted crossings by pulling the cords out from the bottom loop and uncrossing the bottom loop as shown in diagram 6.

Tip
When using double cords to make the knot, if you start with the cords entering the knot on the left side, and finish with the cords emerging on the same (left) side, the two looped cords will fall neatly parallel. However, if you start with the cords entering the knot on the left side and finish with them emerging on the opposite (right) side, the looped cords will be twisted and will need to be untwisted throughout the knot.

12. When you come to the end of the plait, pull the cord through the loop at the bottom.

13. Ensure all the cords are parallel and flat. Tighten the plait.

14. Make a button knot just after the plait, move it into position and thread a brass nut on.

Tip
Thread one cord through the nut, then flatten it down to thread the other cord through.

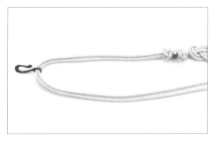

15. Make the next button knot with the longer cord. Thread on the fastener.

Tip
Alternate which piece of cord you use to make the button knots to ensure the lengths end up the same

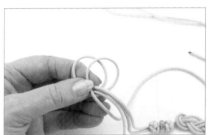

16. Make a button knot with one cord around the other three cords (instructions on page 23).

17. Use the longest cord to make another button knot around three cords and trim and seal the ends. Note that two sliding knots have been made side by side – with this thick cord, a double sliding button knot would have been too bulky.

18. Repeat steps 1–16 for the other side to finish the necklace. Ensure that both sides are the same length.

Button and braid necklaces in different styles, both elegant and rustic.

PLAITS

Interlaced plaits were used as decoration by the ancient Egyptians, Greeks and Romans as well as the Celts. They are probably one of the most ancient designs in existence. Here I show you how to make a three-stranded plait (also known as King Solomon's plait) and a four-stranded plait which results in a wider braid.

Three-stranded plait

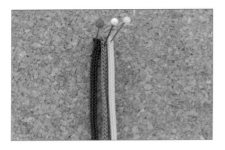

1. Start with three cords, all the same length.

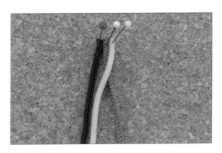

2. Take the right-hand side cord over the middle cord so that it becomes the middle cord.

3. Take the left-hand side cord into the middle.

4. Take the right-hand side cord into the middle.

5. Take the left-hand side cord into the middle.

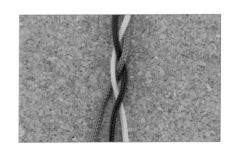

6. Take the right-hand side cord into the middle.

7. Take the left-hand side cord into the middle.

8. Take the right-hand side cord into the middle.

9. Continue until you have your desired length of plait.

Four-stranded plait

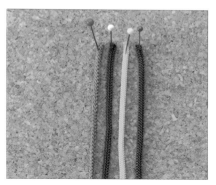

1. Start off with four cords, all of the same length.

2. Take the cord on the right-hand side underneath the next cord to the left, over the next cord and under the last cord on the far left.

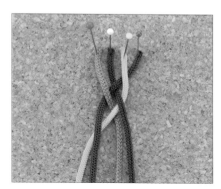

3. Take the cord which is now on the far right (yellow here). Thread it under, then over, and then under the last cord on the left.

4. Take the cord which is now on the far right (deep red here). Thread it under, then over and under the cord on the far left-hand side.

5. Continue until you have your desired length of plait, straightening the plait to keep it vertical as you go along.

31

Plaited necklace with beads

This plait is an extended King Solomon's knot. It is said that all the wisdom of Solomon is contained in this knot, so the plait must contain even more wisdom! The addition of beads in several colours to complement the colour of the cord makes an interesting pattern when plaited. If you thread one third of the beads on to each strand before you start, it does not take very long to make the necklace.

You will need

2m (78in) 1mm cotton cord

1m (39in) 1mm cotton cord

Approximately 130 small glass beads

One larger bead for the closure

1. Fold the 2m (78in) cord in half to make a loop. With one end of the 1m length, make two button knots around the folded 2m cord to create the loop at the end. The longer piece of the 1m (39in) piece of cord makes the third strand of the necklace. Cut off the short end and add a dab of instant glue gel to secure it.

2. Pin the necklace into place and add one third of the beads on to each cord. Leave them on the ends to slide up when needed.

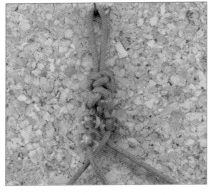

3. Slide each bead up into place before making each crossover. Refer to page 30 if you are unsure of the plaiting method.

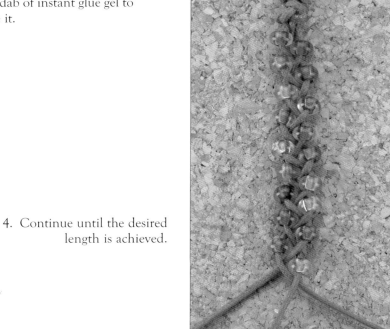

4. Continue until the desired length is achieved.

5. Thread the large bead on to two of the cords, bring the ends around and use one of them to make a button knot around the other three (folded) cords and the remaining cord. Tighten the knot and trim the ends. Add a spot of instant glue gel to secure the ends.

You can use a variety of beads to create different effects for your jewellery.

King Solomon's plait necklace

The medieval name for King Solomon's knot is 'the Emblem of Divine Inscrutability', indicating that at that time, knots did indeed symbolise philosophical meanings. The plaited pattern is clearly visible between the beads, and the contrast in the colour of the cord and beads can be very dramatic, yet the method of making the necklace is very simple. It is a delicate design but much stronger than a necklace threaded in the usual way! It is also an economical way of using up beads that are too few in number to make a simple beaded necklace.

You will need

2m (78in) 1mm cotton cord

1m (39in) 1mm cotton cord, same colour

Twenty-one faceted glass beads

Hook and eye closure

1. Thread the hook closure on to the middle of the 2m (78in) length of cord and fold it in half. Taking the 1m (39in) length of cord, thread one end through the closure for about 6cm (2½in) and use the long end to make a button knot around the other two pieces of cord and the short length. Trim the short end of the cord and secure with instant glue gel.

2. Plait five times (see page 30), then add a bead on the right-hand side cord.

3. Make five more crossovers and add a bead on the right-hand side cord. Continue until you achieve your desired length. You will notice that the beads always fall on the same cord. When you have worked out which cord it is, you can thread the beads on all at once and slide them up as needed.

4. Repeat step 1 for the other end of the necklace, threading on the eye instead of the hook.

Different coloured cords and beads, creating various striking effects.

Four-strand plaited necklace with pendant

The repetition of the plait pattern is reminiscent of the Celtic idea of the ancient rhythm of life, which continues unchanged. Here, leather is used to make the necklace and the plait is wide enough to look attractive with just a pendant to embellish it. It is a good way to use the coloured leather that stores sell already cut into 1m (39in) lengths.

You will need

1.5m (58in) 1.5mm black leather cord

1m (39in) 1.5mm coloured leather

Brass hook and eye closure

Pendant (with jump ring to hang it if needed)

1. Fold the black cord in half, thread the closure on and secure it with a button knot, tying one cord around the other.

2. Fold the coloured length of cord in half and position it underneath the black cord and to the left.

3. Start making a four-stranded plait by bringing the black cord on the right under the coloured cord, over the black and under the coloured on the left (see page 31) and continue until you achieve the desired length.

4. Repeat step 1 for the other end of the necklace, using the eye instead of the hook.

5. Add the pendant, using small pliers to open and close the jump ring to secure it into place.

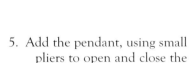

Opposite
The firmness of the leather complements the design of the plait beautifully.

TURK'S HEAD KNOTS

This is a very ancient and elegant knot. The continuous pattern of the Turk's Head knot was regarded by the Christian Celts as a symbol of connection and continuity for eternity. Its name is believed to have originated from the similarity between this knot and a turban.

Turk's Head bangle

The bangle is made with one single cord which is woven around a cylinder to make nine circuits; three to make the basic plait and six more circuits to treble the plait. It is continuous and the join is invisible on the outside. The knot is constructed around a cardboard cylinder about 7cm (2¾in) in diameter. A larger cylinder may be needed depending on the wrist size. You are actually making a three-stranded plait (see page 30) but because the cord is continuous, you make it with one cord at a time instead of three. This bangle has three circuits of the cord plaited over and under each other eleven times to make a total of eleven 'scallops' or curves on each side. Generally the number of 'crossovers' depends on the size of the cylinder you are working around. To make the steps clearer here, I have made the knot around a glass so that you can see the back of the knot as well as the front.

You will need

3m (118in) 2mm braided macramé cord

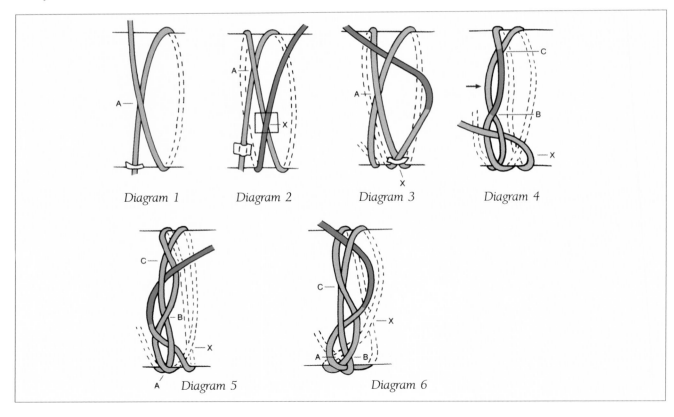

Diagram 1   *Diagram 2*   *Diagram 3*   *Diagram 4*

Diagram 5   *Diagram 6*

1. Imagine that the glass in the photograph is a cardboard cylinder. Stiffen the mobile end of the cord (see page 17). Tape the fixed end of the cord to the left side of the cylinder and make one rotation of the cord, crossing at point A (see diagram 1).

2. Make another rotation of the cord and bring it round to the front in between the two cords already there, crossing over the right-hand cord at point X (see diagram 2). Anchor this crossing temporarily using sticky tape (see bottom of diagram 3) as it tends to uncross during plaiting later on.

3. Thread the cord underneath the top cord on the right-hand side, as in diagram 3.

4. Pull the cord through, in between the two cords. Rotate the cylinder towards you, then cross the left-hand fixed cord over the right-hand one (see diagram 4). The new crossing points are shown as B and C.

5. Take the end of the mobile cord and thread it underneath the left-hand cord and over the right-hand cord between B and C (see diagram 5). You can see that the plait is beginning to take shape.

6. Rotate the cylinder slightly towards you, and above crossing C, thread the mobile end under the right-hand cord (see diagram 6).

7. Repeat step 4.

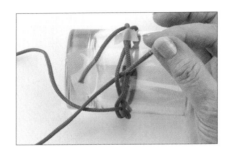

8. Repeat step 5.

9. The cord goes over the right-hand side then above the crossing and underneath the right-hand side cord, as in step 6. Repeat steps 4, 5 and 6 until the desired number of scallops is reached.

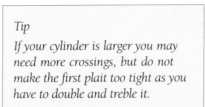

Tip
If your cylinder is larger you may need more crossings, but do not make the first plait too tight as you have to double and treble it.

10. By now, you should have reached your starting point. Follow the path through again to make the plait double.

11. Continue following the cord through until you reach the starting point again. Follow the path around again so that the plait is trebled.

12. Bring the cord ends to the inside and trim the ends off, leaving about 1cm (½in) to be glued down.

13. Seal the ends with a thread zapper or a lighter and secure with instant glue gel. Coat the bangle with diluted PVA glue to keep the shape (see page 14).

You can make your bangle in any colour you wish; see page 18 for instructions on dyeing cords.

Flat Turk's Head pendant

This particular Turk's Head knot is very interesting as it has a six pointed star in its centre which is also known as the Seal of Solomon. It is composed of two triangles, one pointing upwards and the other downwards. The upward pointing triangle is a symbol of fire, (reaching upwards) and the downward pointing one is the symbol of water (as it flows downwards). When combined, the triangles form a potent symbol of balance and divine union. The flat Turk's Head knot makes a lovely pendant, and can also be used to embellish a bangle. In some of the examples I have used acrylic paint to emphasise the star pattern.

You will need

1.2cm (47in) 2mm braided macramé cord

Bead or button for centre (optional)

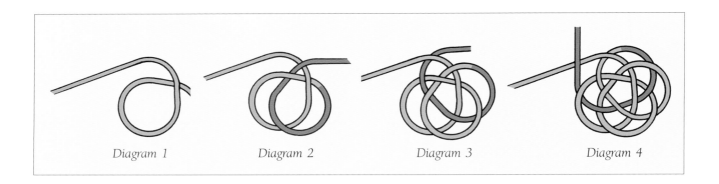

| Diagram 1 | Diagram 2 | Diagram 3 | Diagram 4 |

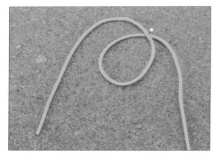

1. Make a loop with the piece of cord and secure with a pin (see Diagram 1). Note the second curve goes under the first curve.

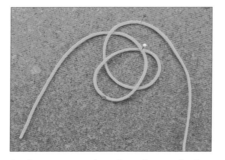

2. Loop around and underneath the previous loop to make another loop (see Diagram 2).

3. Loop around again, taking the end under, then over, under, over then under the looped cords (see diagram 3).

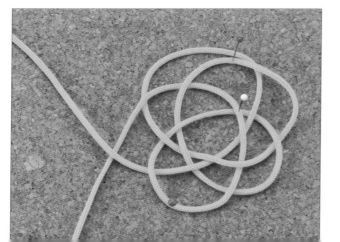

4. Take the cord up and around to create another loop. Take it under, over, under, under, over and under and on top of where the cord started (see diagram 4).

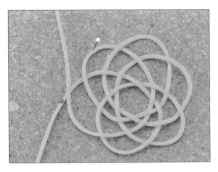

5. Take the cord up and loop around again, taking it under, over, under, over, under, over, under, over and then on top of where the cord started.

6. Tighten the knot.

7. Follow the path of the cord around again to double the knot. You can either trim and seal the ends or use the ends to create a pendant necklace.

You can also use the flat Turk's Head knot to embellish a bangle.

Flat Turk's Head knots, some of which are decorated with acrylic paint to emphasise the star shapes.

Turk's Head ring

This ring is perfect for lovers as it represents the interweaving of their lives and futures. The method of making it shows how easily this knot can be transformed from a flat knot into a circular one.

You will need

78cm (30in) cord

> **Tip**
>
> *Making rings is a marvellous way to use up small ends of cord, though you need at least 52cm (20in) for a double cord ring.*

1. Make a bow shape with the cord and pin it in place.

2. Loop around the bottom, over the cord loop and then under the middle piece of cord.

3. Make another loop and then take the cord under the right-hand side and over, then under and over the bottom right-hand side loop.

4. Make a loop at the bottom and follow the same path as where the cord started from.

5. Follow the loops around to double the lead.

6. Follow the path around again for a treble lead ring.

7. The flat shape makes a lovely pendant, but to make a ring, push the centre through towards you.

8. Continue reshaping the knot, tightening the far side of the ring and loosening the centre as you work.

9. Continue until both sides of the ring are parallel. Secure the ends of the cords in the same way as steps 12–13 on page 40.

The finished rings.

45

FIGURE OF EIGHT CHAINS

The figure of eight pattern is one of the twelve elementary Celtic knots. Although one knot is not self contained in the same way as the Triangular knot or the Circle of Life knot, a chain of figures of eight is made from one continuous line which is also a symbol of eternity – a positive, life-affirming theme in Celtic knotwork. To the Irish scribes of the seventh to ninth centuries, the endless line represented the boundlessness of God.

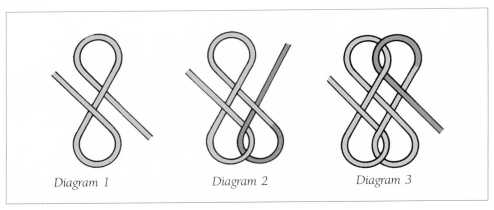

Diagram 1   Diagram 2   Diagram 3

1. Make a figure of eight and pin it in place. Follow the 'overs and unders' shown, as in diagram 1.

2. Loop around to start the next figure of eight and link into the bottom of the first figure of eight (see diagram 2).

3. Loop around to make the top of the eight and link to the top of the previous figure of eight (see diagram 3).

4. Continue making the figures of eight, linking each one into the previous one.

5. Carry on until you have achieved the desired length of chain.

Figure of eight chain bangle

Some say intertwining knots represent the interconnectedness of all life. Others say that they can be devices to bind negativity – it becomes entangled in the knot and cannot escape. Whatever you like to believe, this chain makes a very attractive bangle and is easy to make.

You will need

3m (118in) 2mm cord in turquoise

3m (118in) 2mm cord in purple

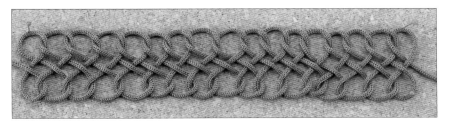

1. Start a figure of eight chain on a cork mat and work about seventeen or eighteen loops.

Tip

The method is shown with only one cord to make the steps easier to follow. To make the bracelet with two colours, weave the second colour in as shown above after step 1.

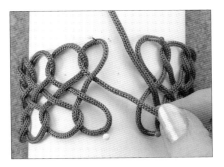

2. Make a cylinder with a sheet of A4 paper, and secure your chain on to it.

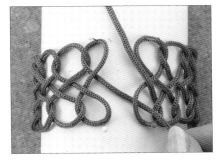

3. Thread the end of the cord on the left-hand side under and through the bottom loop on the right-hand side.

4. Thread it underneath the bottom loop on the left-hand side.

5. Take the end of the cord underneath to make the bottom loop of the figure of eight.

6. The cord then passes over the other end of the cord, under the next loop and over to pass back again.

7. The cord then goes over and under the loop on the left-hand side.

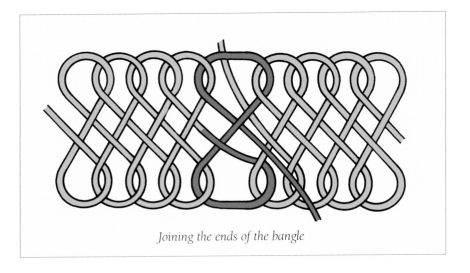

Joining the ends of the bangle

8. Take the cord under the middle of the figure of eight. Trim and seal the ends using a lighter or thread zapper, and secure them on the inside with instant glue gel as in steps 12 and 13 on page 40. Apply PVA glue to the bangle so that it retains its shape.

Opposite

Use various coloured cords to achieve the effect you want.

Horizontal figure of eight chain

The figure of eight is not so easily recognisable when laid on its side, however, its flowing curves make a very attractive and intricate chain.

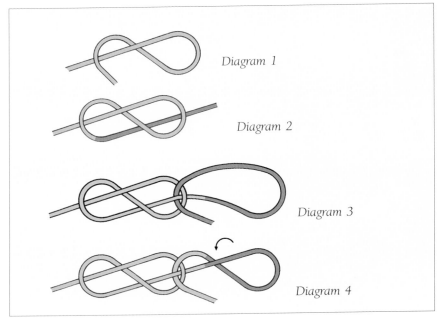

Diagram 1

Diagram 2

Diagram 3

Diagram 4

1. Start the chain with a figure of eight on its side.

2. Take the cord up and underneath the 'eight' towards the top right-hand corner

3. Loop around and over, then under and over again.

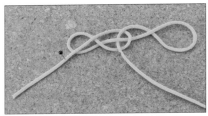

4. Turn the large loop over to form a figure of eight.

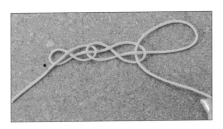

5. Repeat steps 2 and 3, taking the cord end under the loop on the right, then loop back again and then over, under and over again.

6. Repeat steps 4 and 5. When you are satisfied that the chain is the length you want, tuck the free straight cords at the beginning and end through the last loops, as shown in the diagrams.

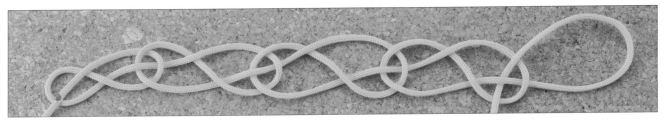

Horizontal figure of eight chain necklace

This horizontal figure of eight chain works up very quickly. Here I have not added any beads, but a pendant could look very nice with it, as you can see on page 53.

You will need

3m (118in) 2mm cord in a natural beige colour

3m (118in) 2mm cord in turquoise

3m (118in) 2mm cord in deep blue

Brass ring and toggle closure

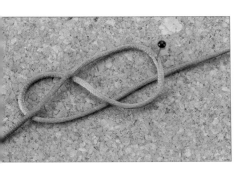

1. Form the first figure of eight using the turquoise cord, leaving enough cord at the end for a button knot and closures on the left-hand side.

2. Loop backwards over the cord, then under and over again as in step 3 on page 50.

3. Following step 4 on page 50, turn the large loop over and repeat steps 2 and 3. Keep building up the chain, adding knots to form the necklace.

Tip

The necklace can be as short or as long as you want. Keep adding knots until you are happy with the length.

4. Add the natural beige cord, leaving a short end at the beginning. This will be threaded through the closure and woven back through the button knot. Follow the path of the turquoise cord, keeping the cords side-by-side. Work the second cord through the length of the necklace.

5. Add in the deep blue cord. Start at the beginning, leaving a long end (this will form the button knot over the turquoise cord). Work the third cord through to the end of the chain.

Tip

The three cord ends will need securing with tape as you move the chain off the cork base. Remove the tape before moving on to step 6.

6. Tuck the free straight cords at the beginning and end of the chain through the last loops. Pass the two blue cords at both ends through the closures after trimming and sealing the beige cord neatly to hide it between the blue cords. Form button knots by working the deep blue cord around the other cords (see page 23). After the button knots are tightened and moved up into the correct place in the design, the ends of the blue cords should be trimmed and sealed neatly.

Opposite

The finished necklace and another example with a pendant. The pendant is secured by weaving the gold cord into the pattern of the necklace, enhancing the design.

INTERLACED KNOTS

Celtic interlacing is almost endless in its variations; it can go in any direction as long as it follows the traditional Celtic knotwork principle of alternate 'overs and unders'.

Celtic cross

This cross is made with two different coloured cords, the tan colour starts at the top of the design and the rust coloured cord starts at the bottom of the cross and becomes part of the necklace.

You will need

2m (78in) 1mm nylon cord in a rust colour

1m (39in) 1mm nylon cord in a tan colour

Two gold Celtic torpedo beads

Brass-coloured hook and eye closure

Diagram 1   Diagram 2

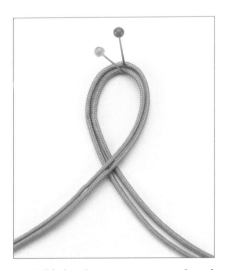

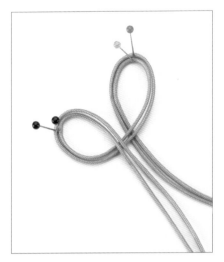

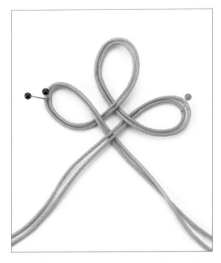

1. Fold the shorter tan piece of cord in half, then fold in half again to make the loop at the top. Pin it in place.

2. Make a loop on the left-hand side and pin it in place. Follow the overs and unders in diagram 1 carefully.

3. Make another loop on the right-hand side and pin it in place.

54

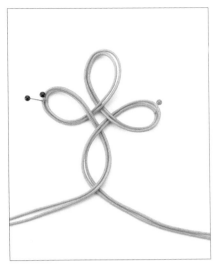

4. Make a loop in the middle, laying the cords on the right-hand side over the cords from the left.

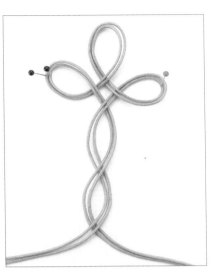

5. Make another loop, again laying the cords from the right-hand side over the cords from the left.

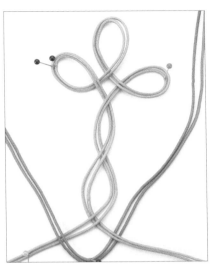

6. Take the rust cord, fold it in half twice as before and pin it into place as shown, starting at the bottom of the cross pattern. The right-hand side rust cords go under the tan cords and the left-hand side rust cords go over the tan cords.

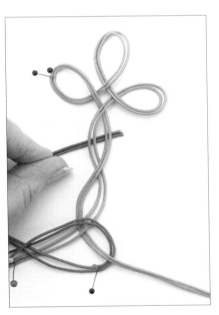

7. Take the right-hand side cords over the cross and then under it.

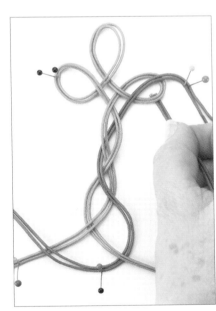

8. Make a loop with the rust cords, pin it in place and thread it under the tan-coloured loop on the right-hand side, following diagram 2.

9. Take the rust cords over themselves then under the top of the right-hand side loop. Continue over the top loop as shown.

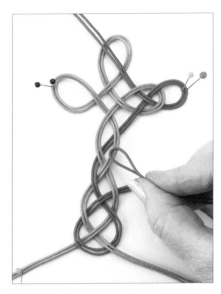
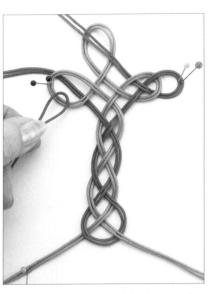

10. Take the rust cords on the left-hand side under the tan cord, over the rust cord and under the tan cord on the right-hand side.

11. Take the rust cord back over the tan cord, under itself, over the tan cord again on the left and under the loop on the left-hand side.

12. Repeat steps 8 and 9 to make the rust loop on the left-hand side. Continue up under the tan loop at the top and over the rust cord, following diagram 2 throughout.

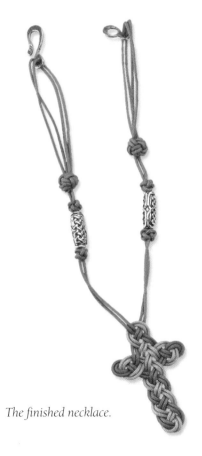

13. Unpin the cross and tighten it. The long rust cords are used to make the rest of the necklace. Trim and secure the tan cords.

14. Add button knots, the gold beads and the closures and secure with sliding double button knots as before.

The finished necklace.

Try different coloured leather cords and beads to create a variety of beautiful cross necklaces.

Circle of Life earrings

The circle is an endless shape and a symbol of eternity. This decorative circle is another Celtic symbol of how all life is intertwined and interconnected.

You will need

Two pieces of 1mm leather cord each 70cm (27in) long
Two beads
Two earring hooks

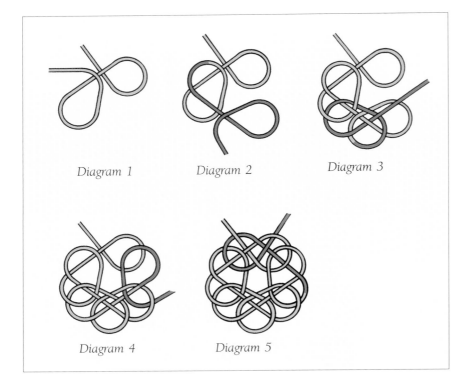

Diagram 1   Diagram 2   Diagram 3

Diagram 4   Diagram 5

Tip
Do not put pins through the leather cord as this will damage it. Secure the cord in place by criss-crossing the pins over the cord.

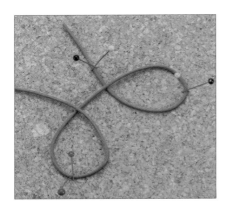

1. Pin the cord into place on the left-hand side and make two loops as shown, following diagram 1.

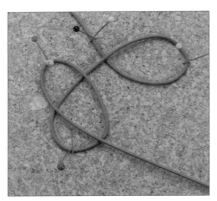

2. Make a loop over the top and pin it in place.

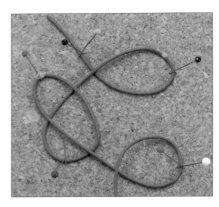

3. Make a loop at the bottom, following diagram 2.

58

4. Make another loop, the same shape as in step 3.

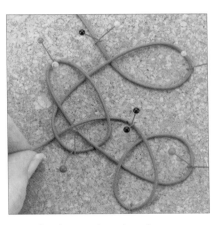

5. Take the cord under, then over and under again as shown.

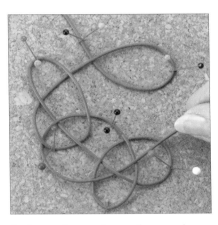

6. Loop the cord round, over, then under and over again, as shown in diagram 3.

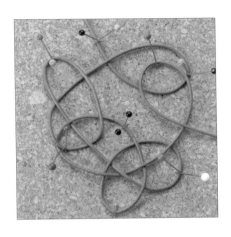

7. Make another loop, laying it on top of the cord already worked.

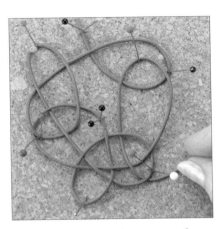

8. Take the cord under, over, under and through as in diagram 4. Pin the loops in place.

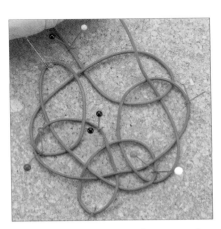

9. Take the cord up and over, under and over again.

10. Take the cord over the top of the top loop and under the cord where you started.

11. Take the cord over, under and over again.

12. Then under, over and under the top of the top loop, as in diagram 5.

13. Take all the pins out and begin to tighten all the knotwork.

Tip
You will know if you have gone wrong as the cords will spring up when the pins are taken out.

14. Tighten the cords as shown.

15. Add the bead and the earring hook and secure with a button knot, trimming and sealing the ends. Then make the other earring.

The Circle of Life knot is perfect for earrings and also makes a neat brooch (inset).

Triangular knot earrings

This knot is also known as a Triquetra, a Celtic symbol of the Triple Goddess. The triple sign was a common symbol in Celtic myth and legend and the idea of three in one is a possible reason why Christian beliefs such as that of the Trinity were so easily adopted by the Celtic people. The sign represented the three domains of the earth, sea and sky, the trinity of mind, body and soul and many other triple concepts as well.

You will need

*Two pieces of 1mm leather cord
each 50cm (20in) long*

Two earring hooks

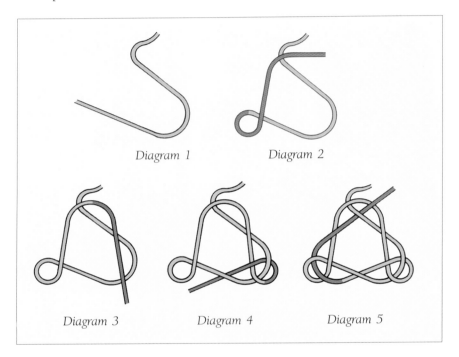

Diagram 1   Diagram 2

Diagram 3   Diagram 4   Diagram 5

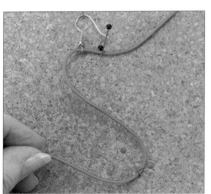

1. Thread the earring hook on to the cord to about half way and secure it with pins. Make an S-shaped loop as in diagram 1 and pin it in place.

2. Loop around and back up to the top, as in diagram 2.

3. Pin the shape in place.

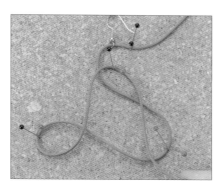

4. Loop back round and down, as in diagram 3.

5. Loop around the outside edge, underneath the outside and over the centre and under the bottom cord, as in diagram 4.

6. Thread the cord through the loop on the left-hand side as shown.

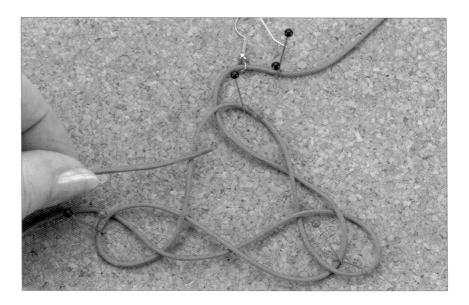

7. Bring the cord back over, near the top of the earring.

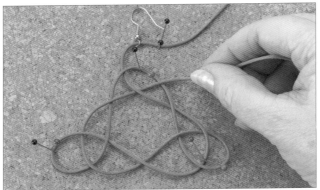

9. Go back round to the left and follow the path of the cord again to make the knot double thickness. Trim and secure the ends as shown on page 40.

8. Then under and over again on the right-hand side, as in Diagram 5.

Finished triangular knot earrings, incorporating the Celtic symbol of the Triple Goddess.

Two heart brooch

The heart shape is universally considered to be an expression of love. It is a relatively new symbol and would not have been in use in the time of the early Christian Celts. However, its inclusion in the vocabulary of symbolic knotwork shows that Celtic artwork is a living and evolving tradition.

The diagram of the knot pattern showing the path of the cords and the way they are threaded alternately over and under each other. Photocopy the diagram and pin it to your cork mat. If you want to use a thicker cord, you will need to enlarge the diagram on a photocopier first.

You will need

1.5m (59in) 1mm nylon cord in dark red

Three pieces of 1mm pink nylon cord, each 1.5m (59in) long

Brooch bar

Small piece of thin leather same size as brooch bar

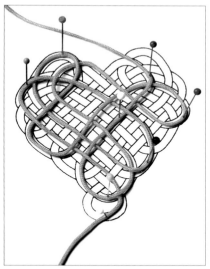

1. Find the middle of the cord and pin it to the centre of the bottom loop on the diagram. Following the guide lines, pin the right half of the cord over or under the crossings as shown on the diagram. Continue until the top of the heart is reached.

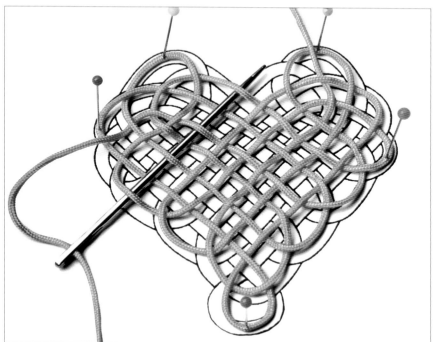

2. Weave the left side of the cord through with a smooth tipped tapestry needle, following the diagram.

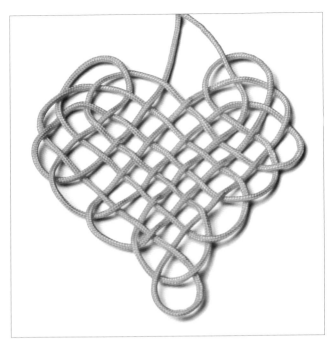

3. When you have completed the heart with one cord, unpin it. Any mistakes will be apparent, as the cord will spring up.

4. Weave in the second cord, following the lead of the first cord, starting at the bottom and using the tapestry needle as before.

5. Tighten all the cords as shown above. Make another heart knot using only pink cord and following the steps shown above.

6. Trim and secure the end of the cords neatly using instant glue gel. Glue the brooch pin to a small thin piece of leather and then stick this on to the two-tone heart with instant glue gel. Attach the pink heart to the first heart using small spots of instant glue gel.

You can use the heart knot to make a variety of jewellery.

Josephine knot necklace

This is an ancient Celtic knot that has been popular for thousands of years. It can be found in various cultures, each of which has a different name for the knot. Josephine is a relatively recent name, after Napoleon Bonaparte's Empress. Since there is ample evidence that early Celtic society was matriarchal, it is appropriate to use the name here. In this necklace the knots are linked from side to side and made using just one continuous cord – an unusual style and very attractive. The beaded scallops stabilise the necklace design.

You will need

4m (160in) 2mm
black cotton cord

1.5m (59in) 1mm
black cotton cord

130 assorted colour
glass beads

Hook and eye closure

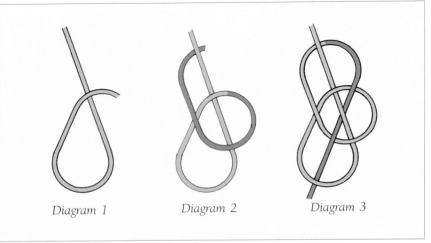

Diagram 1   *Diagram 2*   *Diagram 3*

1. Make a loop with the 2mm cotton cord (see diagram 1) and pin it in place.

2. Make another loop on top, and slightly to the right (see diagram 2).

3. Cross the cord over and then under as shown.

4. Loop around and over, then under, over and under.

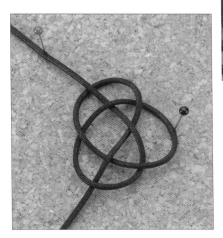

5. Pull the cord through so the knot takes shape as above (see diagram 3). Repeat steps 1–5 to make another knot below the first one. Continue until you have made about twelve knots.

6. Take the length of thinner cord and tie a larkshead knot (shown above) to the top Josephine knot in the necklace.

7. Add about nine beads to the short end of the thin cord and pin it in place as shown.

8. Add about eleven beads to the next scallop and loop through the next Josephine knot as shown to begin another larkshead knot.

10. Bring the cord underneath the loop to finish the larkshead knot. Continue until you have added beaded scallops to each Josephine knot, adding eleven beads each time.

9. Loop the thinner cord through the Josephine knot again.

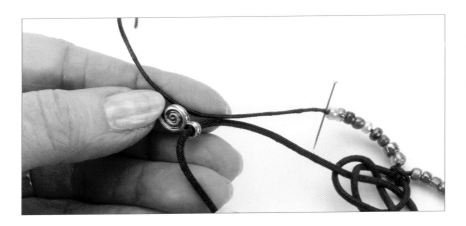

11. Add nine beads to the end of the thinner cord after the last larkshead knot. Secure them with a pin as shown. Thread the closure on to the thicker piece of cord.

12. With the end of the thicker cord, make a button knot around the thin cord and the two cords to secure. Tighten the button knot, then cut and secure the thin cord with instant glue gel to stop it slipping out.

13. Repeat steps 11 and 12 for the other end of the necklace, using the hook fastener instead of the eye.

Jospehine knots create intricate patterns, perfect for necklaces and bracelets. The necklace and bracelet in black and the blue necklace with the turquoise pendant were also made with Josephine knots, but the series of knots were made in the more traditional vertical style, starting with the cord folded in half, and the knots made with the two cord ends, one on each side.

Celtic square knot necklace

To the monks of early Christianity, the square symbolised the creation of the manifold universe. They used the geometric method of construction to create knots to fill squares in their designs for embellishing manuscripts. This knot fits into a square, although here we have adapted it to make a necklace with a pendant so the shape has become slightly elongated. Knots made with cord (compared to knots constructed geometrically on paper) have a life of their own!

You will need

3m (118in) silver coloured 2mm satin cord

3m (118in) turquoise 2mm braided cord

One Celtic silver circular pendant

Two Celtic spangle hexagonal silver beads

Six Celtic oval silver beads

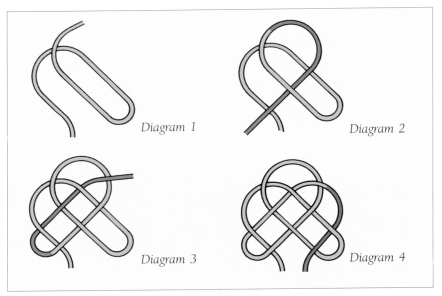

Diagram 1

Diagram 2

Diagram 3

Diagram 4

1. Find the middle of the silver cord and fold the cord in half at this point. Tie a larkshead knot around the Celtic pendant.

2. Make a loop with the cord on the left-hand side (see diagram 1).

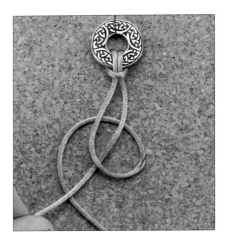

3. Take the right-hand side cord and thread it over, under and over the other cord (see diagram 2).

4. Loop the cord around, taking it up and under, over then under (see diagram 3).

5. Loop the cord around the top, take it under and then over, following diagram 4. Tidy the knot, making sure it is symmetrical.

6. Find the middle of the turquoise cord, pin it in place as shown and start to follow the path of the silver cord around again.

7. Finish following the path of the first knot with the turquoise cord.

8. Make a button knot with the silver cord around the other three cords. Then make two button knots further down with the turquoise cord.

9. Continue adding beads and knots as shown.

10. Finish with two sliding double button knots.

The finished necklace.

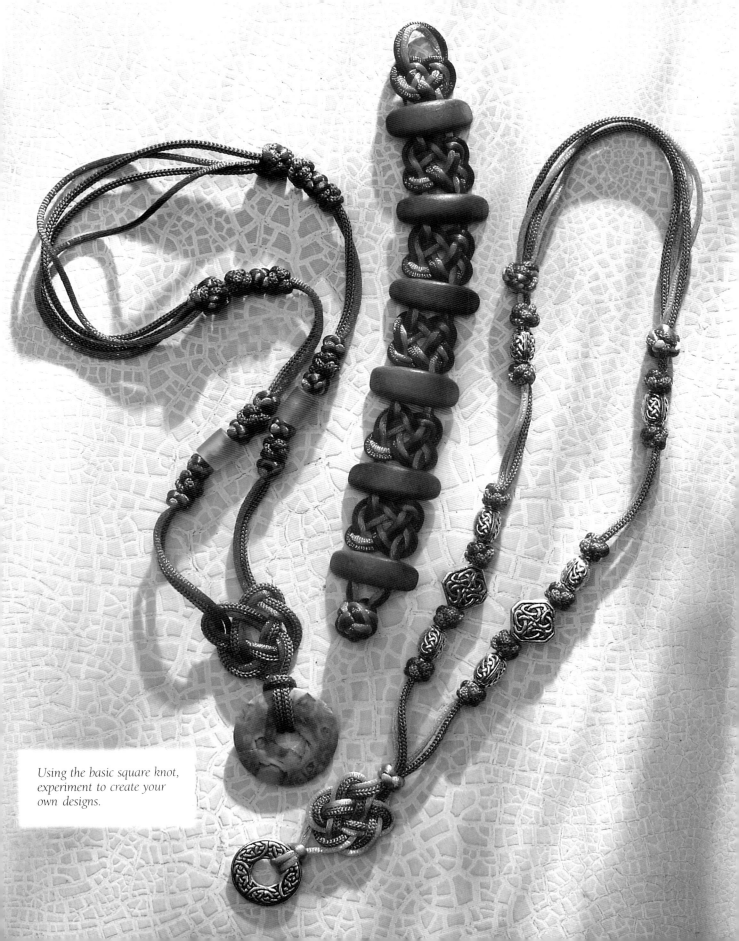

Using the basic square knot, experiment to create your own designs.

Rectangular Celtic knot necklace

The rectangular knot is just an extended square knot and this knot is constructed of several Josephine knots intertwined one after the other. If the pattern is extended even further it would become a Josephine knot border, another example of the versatility of Celtic knots. Here the knot combines beautifully with a silver pendant.

You will need

3m (118in) light red 2mm satin cord

3m (118in) dark red 2mm satin cord

Large silver pendant

Two Celtic spangle (hexagonal) silver beads

Four Celtic lozenge silver beads

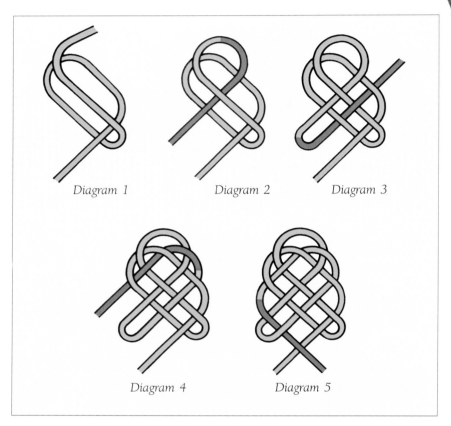

Diagram 1 *Diagram 2* *Diagram 3*

Diagram 4 *Diagram 5*

1. Thread the cords through the pendant loop until the pendant is half way along. Loop the light red cord and pin into place.

2. Loop the cord around, under and through as in diagram 1.

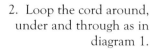

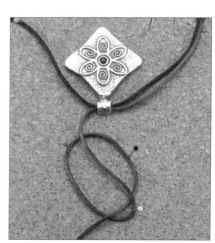

3. Take the light red cord on the right-hand side, loop it around and pin it into place, over, under and over the first loops, as in diagram 2.

4. Loop down, around and underneath, then over and under towards the top right as shown (see diagram 3).

5. Loop around the top, over the cord, under, over and under and through to the other side (see diagram 4). I have moved the black pin to secure the loop in place.

6. Bring the cord down, over then under and through to the bottom, laying it over the other cord (see diagram 5).

7. Follow the path of the light red cord with the dark red cord.

8. Tighten the knot.

9. Make two button knots, the first with the light red cord and the second with the dark red cord.

10. Add, button knots, beads and sliding double button knots as shown.

Opposite

Beautiful silver Celtic beads complement this knot perfectly for the red necklace, and the luxurious bracelet is made with a combination of square and rectangular Celtic knots and silver beads and findings.